This book belongs to

....

Cellotude

Cellotude
A fast track to brilliance

Sara Lovell

BEAUTIFULBOOKS

First published 2006.

Beautiful Books Limited
117 Sugden Road
London SW11 5ED

www.beautiful-books.co.uk

ISBN 1905636024/9781905636020

9 8 7 6 5 4 3 2 1

Text and illustrations copyright © Sara Lovell 2006
Designed and produced by nlAtelier.
Printed in the Czech Republic by Finidr.

The right of Sara Lovell to be identified as the author of this work has been asserted by her in accordance with the Copyright, Designs and Patents Act 1988.

All rights reserved. No part of this publication may be reproduced, stored in or introduced into a retrieval system, or transmitted, in any form, or by any means (electronic, mechanical, photocopying, recording or otherwise) without the prior written permission of the publisher. Any person who does any unauthorised act in relation to this publication may be liable to criminal prosecution and civil claims for damages.

A catalogue reference for this book is available from the British Library.

Acknowledgement

I would like to thank *Colin Irving* and *Vivien Arthur* for their support; three of my long-suffering students, *Jennifer*, *Sarah* and *Hugh*; and *all* of the students, teachers, youth orchestras, music schools and colleges that helped me with my research in 2002-2003.

In particular I would like to thank *Geoff Merrigan*, as without his help, expertise and patience this little book might never have been completed.

I would also like to thank my white cat, *Dimitri*, who has in his lifetime modelled *all* the cat poses for the illustrations in this booklet.

Sara Lovell

To Dori Dawes and Sara Sharpe,

with love.

CELLOTUDE

THIS IS AN excellent booklet for cellists. However, it does not only apply to cellists but to all young people learning string instruments. It is full of wonderful suggestions and I believe that it would be of great value to any young string player, helping them to achieve confidence with a positive and constructive approach to playing. One senses Sara's enthusiasm for music and performance in every paragraph. The presentation is very good and her ideas are presented in a very concise and clear way. It all makes great sense.
Professor David Strange, Head of Strings,
Royal Academy of Music

CONGRATULATIONS TO SARA on providing such an informative and easily digestable publication, which I think will be of great benefit to every budding cellist, their teachers and perhaps especially their parents too. It is so important that aspiring young musicians have a very positive experience yet the upbeat, but highly informative, approach of this book is one which I greatly applaud.
Stephen Threlfall, Director of Music,
Chetham's School of Music

Critical reviews

LEARNING A MUSICAL instrument plays a critical, even vital, role in the development of any child given that opportunity. The progress that is stimulated, from individual skill and its practice to the social aspects of working in an ensemble, cannot be underestimated, and continues to inspire (and surprise!) those who teach. This little book is full of useful advice and practical suggestion. It contains pointers to the pupil and, dare I say, reminders to the teacher. The most important thing is that much of the information it contains is applicable to other instruments, even other disciplines.
Peter Stark, Conductor

A LOVELY, ENTERTAINING contribution to the cello literature, filled with good practical advice. I especially enjoyed the information on posture, tension and relaxation – really wonderful and well-researched ideas.
Paul Marleyn, Professor of Cello,
University of Ottawa, Canada

CELLOTUDE

THIS IS AN excellent little book based on sound principles and tested theories. It offers specific advice to both students of the cello and their parents but the general principles are applicable to a much wider readership, regardless of whether they are a musician or not. All of us will recognize within this book our own shortcomings when trying to achieve our best intentions and Sara offers comforting and constructive advice on how to overcome this. She explains how to organize one's thinking in order to gain a really positive mental attitude – surely the key to real success in performance. An easy to read book that will engage enthusiasm, improve organisation and build confidence. I thoroughly recommend it to students, teachers and the world in general.

Jonathan Vaughan, Director,
National Youth Orchestra of Great Britain

Critical reviews

I AM SURE Sara's concise and focused book will be of immense help to all young instrumentalists. It addresses problems and provides answers in a most approachable manner and should become a *'must have'* for all young string players. Her enthusiasm and obvious love of teaching and learning will be of great value to all who are engaged in this process. I heartily endorse this valuable addition to our teaching literature.

Malcolm Layfield, Head of School of Strings,
Royal Northern College of Music

THIS HAPPY LITTLE handbook should be helpful to students, teachers and parents. Building confidence while developing a positive attitude and approach to achievement is a lifelong aspiration. This is an excellent start.

Marin Alsop, Music Director
Baltimore Symphony Orchestra

CELLOTUDE

Contents

Handling learning — 1

The Twelve Rules — 11

How to make your cello sound really expensive — 19

Are you sitting comfortably — 27

Cellotude in practice — 45

CELLOTUDE

HANDLING LEARNING

The development of Cellotude

CELLOTUDE

Handling learning

You can begin to learn quickly, efficiently, and most importantly, *enjoyably* – when you've given yourself a good talking to!

Many students have the most awful hang-ups about learning, and sometimes just about taking advice. Emma, one of the most gifted students that I have worked with, would get a form of stage fright in the lesson and was practically tying herself up in knots if I said that something could be still better. It was as if the coaching was saying that something was wrong with her *as a person*. As a consequence she would tense up totally; and found it extremely difficult to apply the suggested improvements, which made her feel worse and worse.

How many times have we been our own worst enemy when it comes to learning, or improving, quickly? The teacher gives us a huge chance to make something sound better (whether it's more efficient bowing, fingering, or a specific way of approaching a phrase or piece), and instead of simply applying the suggested change, we start filling our heads with so much baggage – as if we were about to go off on holiday somewhere! "He/she must think I'm such an idiot/why didn't I think of that before/ if I'd worked harder this wouldn't be such a problem/I'll never sort this one out as quickly as he/she wants – they'll be annoyed with me."

> Rules and models destroy genius and art.
> *William Hazlitt*

Do you see the personal negative spiral beginning? Imagine – if you had someone stood next to you criticising in that way, would you stand for it? Now, imagine trying to focus on applying a challenging finger change or whatever wading through that lot, and before you know it you'll be up to your neck in emotional deep water… Perhaps the time has come to make sure that we apply the same standards inside our head as outside.

Handling learning

Teachers aren't mind readers. They cannot and should not attempt to *completely* understand anyone because we all have unique life experiences and ways of thinking... The brilliant news is, though, that both they and you are able to stop that negative spiral from even starting in the first place!

The good teacher will always give pointers that are directly related to the *playing*, not the person. All you need to do is to bear the following tips in mind:

CELLOTUDE

- *You're paying to enjoy learning the cello – not to have a gruelling counselling session...*

- *Both you and the teacher will want your playing to improve as rapidly as possible...*

- *The best players move fluidly, in a relaxed manner, even when the music is at its most demanding musically and/or technically. So relax.*

- *Listen out for tips – and ask for them. After all, you're the one who is paying for the time!*

- *And finally, how you bow, finger, or phrase during the lesson will have absolutely no bearing on whether the world loves you or not, so you might as well smile as you begin to relax – and enjoy making music!*

> When you can't solve the problem, manage it.
>
> Robert Schuller

Handling learning

- *Henry Ford once said that if you want to increase your success rate then you must be prepared to increase your number of mistakes. Celebrate them – they will simply take you closer to your goal if you enjoy learning from them.*

You can expect to be criticised if you wish – but how about having the far better feeling if you go in to a lesson expecting some praise; and then *get* it? If you think like this, notice –

how much more relaxed would that make you feel? And how much more easily would you be able to take all those useful tips and put them *immediately* to good use?

I remember some terrible lessons at Music College, when as a teenager I was hard-wired into taking everything personally. If one so-called 'bad' lesson or masterclass took place, I would expect the next one to go the same way – irrespective of how much practice I had done. What was weird was that I found praise even harder to take, especially when I was expecting criticism – what a waste of a good time; particularly as there was, and is, a far more efficient and fun way to learn!

In contrast, I overheard one of my teenage students recently, singing softly to herself as she took her cello out of its case. She looked and sounded both happy and relaxed, and, although it was merely a scale that she was singing, it was really obvious that she had already focussed

Handling learning

the sound in her mind – way before she actually started to tune up the cello. In short, she was really looking forward to the lesson, which, as I remember, went spectacularly well. She was really buzzing by the end, and still singing on her way up the garden path afterwards (not a scale this time, but a piece that we had only just started that day)! This is a fabulous attitude to have, or, as many of my students now call it, *cellotude*... This concept turns a lesson into a whole new experience, with far-reaching consequences and benefits, especially where confidence is concerned.

> When we build, let us think that we build for ever.
>
> *John Ruskin*

So, the vital questions are really — firstly, *when* do you want to dramatically improve as a player? And secondly, *when* do you next want to have the *cellotude* to expect to receive praise for your playing? Now or…

THE TWELVE RULES FOR

a happy cello

CELLOTUDE

A happy cello

— 1 —

Never leave the cello unattended in a car. *Cellos get stolen very easily, and you will need to make special arrangements with your insurance company if you wish to leave it unattended for any length of time.*

— 2 —

If it's a hot day and the cello is in the car, cover the case with a blanket; it keeps things (much) cooler if you've got a long journey. *You can then avoid expensive problems such as wood warping, varnish melting, seams coming unglued etc.*

> The less you know, the more confident you are.
>
> *Chinese proverb*

– 3 –

Always keep the cello (and bow) out of direct sunlight. *Crazed and 'melted' varnish can drastically affect the look of your investment, not to mention problems such as in 2) above.*

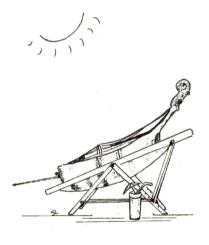

– 4 –

Keep your cello (and bow) away from radiators. *See 2 above.*

A happy cello

— 5 —

Avoid touching the horsehair on the bow. *Grease from hands will make both the hair and the rosin useless.*

— 6 —

Avoid touching the strings between the fingerboard and the bridge. *Grease from hands will stop the friction needed for making a sound.*

— 7 —

After practising, if you're not doing more that day, the cello will be safer in its case. Otherwise leave it on its side, with the spike in, covered with a soft cloth. *(But watch out if animals are about, or clumsy humans!)*

– 8 –

To begin with, rosin the bow every two days; you won't need more – *yet!* However, as you progress, you'll rapidly find that you need to rosin the bow every time you practise.

> Experience is one thing you can't get for nothing.
>
> *Oscar Wilde*

– 9 –

Clean the strings after every practice with a soft dry duster. Some people prefer to use spirit every two days (surgical spirit on a duster or better still, eau de Cologne – it smells **so** much nicer). If in doubt, ask your teacher. *If you use spirit, be careful to clean only the strings, not the cello, or you'll take off the varnish! Use a different, clean duster for that.*

A happy cello

– 10 –

It is a great help if you can get spare strings (the same make that you have already) to keep in your cello case. *Then you can still enjoy playing if a string breaks by putting on a new one right away.*

– 11 –

In order to get new music, ring a good music shop that does a *fast* postal service – *not* somewhere that will take at least two weeks!

The better the cello, the better the case should be, especially if you are travelling about with it to any great extent. Make sure that the cello is well protected, and remember that shock can do just as much damage as an actual knock to an instrument.

Soft cases are lighter and much cheaper, but bridges and pegs can easily be knocked or nudged out of place making this a somewhat suspect economy. Never leave cellos standing unsupported in hard (or soft) cases as they are liable to topple – they do much better on their sides.

> The fool wonders, the wise man asks.
> *Benjamin Disraeli*

HOW TO MAKE YOUR CELLO

sound really expensive

CELLOTUDE

Make your cello sound really expensive

TIPS AND TRICKS OF THE PROFESSIONALS

To make your average cello sound as if it's worth *far* more:

> That rarest gift to beauty, common sense.
> *George Meredith*

— 1 —

Take it to a good luthier (cello maker) who will check the set-up of the cello. All too often, cellos have a badly made, substandard bridge that's incorrectly positioned, at the wrong height, and possibly warped! Soundpost and tailpiece positioning can also be sorted out, as they are part and parcel of the set-up too. A tailpiece that has adjusters for tuning *incorporated* is a very good idea, as with less moving parts there is less of a chance of unwelcome buzzes when you play!

CELLOTUDE

— 2 —

Use good strings. With strings, you get what you pay for – opt for the best steel strings that you can (they are easier to tune). For an extra £30 you will get a richer sound with *no* effort from you! Replce them every year or so, depending on how much you play.

Make your cello sound really expensive

> **Whatever you are be a good one.**
> *Abraham Lincoln*

– 3 –

Use good rosin. Rosin, derived from resin, works in exactly the same way as quality strings (you get what you pay for), and can be made to last for years. Cheap rosin tends to be coarse, and cakes easily on the string, leading to a sound not too unrelated to a cat or a scratched record. Smooth bow changes become well nigh impossible, no matter how good you are, or how hard you work at it. BUT… for an extra fiver you can have fine-ground rosin that will create a silky sound and bow-change for next to no effort.

> I am the way I am. That's the way I'm made.
> *Jaques Prévert*

— 4 —

Use rosin sparingly every practice and handle like eggs... If you put *loads* on the bow hair, it'll get caked. It's better not to lend out rosin, as it is all too easy to drop it (rosin has two principal wishes in life – to break; or to accidentally go off on holiday with someone

> Such sweet compulsion doth in music lie.
> *John Milton*

else) or for yourself or another cellist to stand on it! Do remember to keep your fingers off the cake of rosin (likewise the horsehair on the bow and the area of the strings between the fingerboard and the bridge), as hands are *greasy*. Horsehair is made up of lots of little barbs that stand up when rosin is applied, creating a good friction and playing surface. Grease makes the barbs flatten and is akin to putting soap on the bow – you can do your best, but no sound will be forthcoming!

Make your cello sound really expensive

— 5 —

Clean your strings. Usually a wipe with a clean, dry duster on the area of the strings between the bridge and the fingerboard will do the trick. Otherwise Surgical Spirit on a piece of kitchen roll works wonders and takes off any severe residue or caking, which can affect your sound. *Note: keep spirit away from the actual wood or you'll take off the varnish too...* If you would prefer to have your cello smell less like a dentists, you can opt to use eau de toilette (I discovered this as a teenager — *sorry mum*) or brandy, which doesn't work quite so well but is extremely useful if you're in a fix!

CELLOTUDE

ARE YOU

sitting comfortably?

CELLOTUDE

Sitting comfortably?

Head

Did you know that your head weighs about the same amount as a bowling ball? That's some weight, isn't it — but if it's perfectly balanced on the top of your neck and back, there's no need to notice it (even when rotating/turning), and the muscles in your neck can afford to have some degree of relaxation.

However, the moment that the head tips forward out of balance, the muscles in the neck are forced to take up the strain, possibly having to work *on top of* other requirements, such as playing the cello.

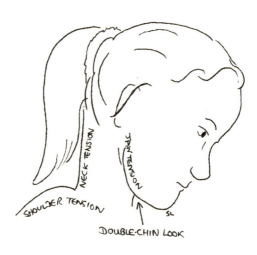

Sitting comfortably?

If you're right in the middle of the powerful first page of the Dvorak cello concerto at the time, there may be trouble ahead, with you in agony before the end of the first movement! Many players have been unconsciously doing this for years; next time you go to an orchestral concert, look out for dipping heads and stiff necks – rounded shoulders – or a stoop...

Feel the tension...

Instead, imagine yourself sitting up under a waterfall allowing the top of your head to push up against the flow of water keeping an upright posture.

Standing Tall

Important: when you relax your fine motor control and sensitivity are greatly increased.

Sitting comfortably?

Shoulders

Shoulders never stop working when you're playing! Rather than go into the particular muscles used, it's easier to show where the biggest tension points are – namely, between shoulder and neck. If these are already in tension (from trying to maintain the position of your head, worry, etc) they have conflicting tasks.

ARROWS SHOWING TENSION AREAS...

For any physiotherapist reading this the muscles are being asked to simultaneously abduct, adduct, rotate, extend *and* flex…, and are more likely to tire or go into spasm easily ("bow shake" is a common example of a result of this problem in action.)

> A wise man sees his own faults,
> a courageous man corrects them.
> *Chinese proverb*

If, however, they're allowed to move freely, you'll get terrific action for very little effort, backed up by your now more relaxed arm and hand muscles. It also means that your breathing is less restricted so you will have more energy for the longer passages… win, win and win!

Breathing

If you don't breathe, apart from getting tired more easily and actually inducing tension in your body, it won't look or sound good.

> If thy heart fails thee, climb not at all.
> *Queen Elizabeth I*

It's amazing how we all like to hold our breath when we approach what we perceive to be a 'difficult' passage or task, isn't it? And yet, if we're to use really fine, quick muscle movements, our brains are going to need a *very* good supply of oxygen to send out the necessary motor messages to our hands and fingers that are needed. If we restrict breathing (by taking shallow breaths, contracting the neck muscles, rounding the shoulders, slouching or simply holding our breath) the fine movements are always the first casualties.

Watch out for pulling faces as you play – it's a sure-fire indicator.

Going blue... fast

Middle and Lower Back

It's important to be sitting upright (remember the waterfall) when playing. Using a wedge cushion, or else blocks to raise the back legs of the chair is a good idea because it causes your

Sitting comfortably?

pelvis to sit in such a way that your back retains its natural shape more efficiently.

Stomach muscles should be doing *their* bit to keep you upright, not just leaving everything to the back muscles. Imagine sitting with two hands on your hips, supporting you and keeping you straight while you play. You can rock/rotate from side to side as much as you like, *as long as* your trunk returns to straight!

'Hugged' by rhythm...

Think: natural shape = natural sound

> Only the very knowledgable and the
> very ignorant do not shift their ground.
> *Confucius*

Sitting comfortably?

Legs and Feet
Legs should be bent, with feet just behind your knees, facing forward. Feet may be flat on the floor (for smaller people this can be a real problem on adult-sized chairs), but more importantly, you should feel that the balls of your feet are taking the most weight, and that you have the ability to jump up at any time.

Occupational Hazard...

Have you ever tried playing barefoot?

Hands and Arms

Your muscles work in opposing pairs; that is, there is always a muscle resisting any movement or action. So, if you are tense, then it is easy to imagine the extra work required for any movement. It's not always necessary to use both sets of muscles *(for example, while raising your arm)* and it's easy to give one group a rest whilst using another.

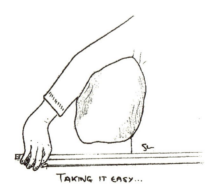

TAKING IT EASY...

You can hold your left elbow up while you play so much more easily if you imagine that there's an imaginary cushion supporting it – in short,

Sitting comfortably?

using the same principle as Chi Kung, the ancient martial art.

> Concentration is the secret of strength.
> *Ralph Emerson*

Remember your bow hand works just like a hinge to let the bow move across the string – *as freely and as straight as you wish*. You can grip a bow as hard as you like, but it takes much less effort just to guide the thing and feel it move easily through your fingers!

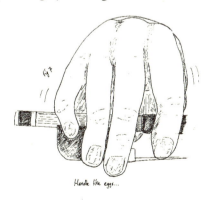

Handle like eggs...

Your left hand can equally throttle the neck of the cello if it wants to, but if you want to get the instrument to sing sweetly, this is to be avoided! All your fingers need to do is to get the string onto the fingerboard enough to focus the pitch and the sound whilst your finger remains rounded.

When it feels as if that's way too easy, and it sounds good, you've probably got it right.

You can get your left thumb to collapse on itself and grip manically — but it's *so* much easier to let your thumb stay rounded, and relax where it wants, merely positioning itself to aid the fingers!

It's wrong to say that the left thumb must go 'here' or 'there' as every thumb is a different size and shape, but somewhere in between the first and second finger is a good place to start. Also, if you're playing on the top (A) string, the thumb will be further round the neck than if you're playing on the bottom (C) string.

Sitting comfortably?

A final word of warning – if your cello spike (endpin) is not properly secured so that it doesn't skid forward/left or right, all your best intentions will come to nothing as the instrument starts to behave like a wild animal and all but struggles to escape from you! The amount of tension needed to keep that cello from

> Faith, thou hast some crotchets in thy head now.
>
> William Shakespeare

scuttling off from you is truly *amazing*! The spike can badly damage carpets and wooden floors too, which could prove to be potentially very expensive for you. Use a spike guard, or better still, a T-square (the latter is a little awkward to carry, *but* it does a perfect job and is ever so cheap to make).

CELLOTUDE

Experiment and have fun.

CELLOTUDE

in practice

CELLOTUDE

Approach to practice

As with many things, its terribly easy to start playing with every good intention of doing x amount of playing every day – and then, a day gets missed, which becomes two, then possibly three. And then, it's suddenly the following week and the next lesson is tomorrow, so in a fit of guilt or fear (the latter if one's on a music scholarship somewhere!) the student does a huge practice and then forgets most if not all of it in the lesson, to the annoyance of the student, the teacher, and very definitely the person who's footing the bill!

Unfortunately this sort of thing can happen again, and again, until regretfully the student packs it in as a bad job as the missiles of blame and shame start to fly, wounding anything that they ricochet off or strike.

So, in the hope of avoiding all that heartache, here are some pointers that many successful students and I have found to be particularly useful in developing a realistic, strong and *positive* approach to playing.

> I feel a feeling which I feel you all feel.
> *Bishop George Ridding*

– 1 –

Make it a priority to play little *and* often – did you know that 95% of true practice is done *away* from the cello (and that it's possible to memorise the entire cello part of a concerto on the train from, say, London to Manchester)? When you're actually playing, it's *far* better to concentrate hard for three fifteen-minute bursts than it is to play for an hour straight.

– 2 –

Ask yourself, realistically, what you are prepared to *give up* to achieve the level of skill that you want. If you want to simply get around the instrument and join the local orchestra,

In practice

then fine, it may be possible to fit the practice in with work plus Computer Club on Tuesday, swimming on Wednesday, judo on Thursday, ballet on Friday and a sleepover at the weekend. If, on the other hand, you want to win prizes, scholarships and auditions – something's got to give way to the cello.

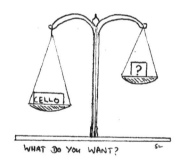

WHAT DO YOU WANT?

– 3 –

Parents and guardians – outside involvement is *essential* for youngsters. They need to be encouraged, to know *why* they are playing, *what* the immediate as well as the long distance goals are, and *how* to achieve that within the practice time available. We always hear about the occasional parent and/or guardian who can be terribly pushy. The truth is that there are at least treble those numbers who are so laid back about challenging the children in their care that they're quite literally falling over in the duty.

> Talent develops in quiet places, character in the full current of human life.
> *Johann von Goethe*

It is extremely difficult for a child to get excited about playing if that's the attitude from above. It's so easy to bow out and say 'but I don't know anything about music – how can *I* help?' whereas most supportive mums, dads and guardians will make *every* effort to understand the 'offside' rule if little Johnny has the chance of playing footie for the County! *Support* is the key word here – show a big genuine interest, and the benefits will be huge.

In practice

> Victory belongs to the persevering.
> *Napoleon Bonaparte*

Go in and listen to some part of the practice, or the result of that day's attempts. The cello is not just a solo instrument! Get your charge into an orchestra or into chamber music (trios, quartets etc) as soon as possible so that friendships are quickly made with other young musicians. Peer pressure is not to be sniffed at, and you can swap some *very* useful ideas/lifts/addresses with other parents and guardians too! Never think that because you don't know much about music you will look stupid.

— 4 —

Practice time, as I mentioned in (1) is best done in three short bursts, once or twice a day (if you're a music student it can be three or four times). Set the time by; write it on a planner and *stick* to it.

CELLOTUDE

> Three o'clock is always too late or too early for anything you want to do.
> *Jean-Paul Sartre*

It's obviously better to use a time when you're pretty wide-awake! If you're a lark, then go for the morning if possible. If you're a night owl, then perhaps check with the neighbours first! It's always possible to negotiate playing time – how easily you manage this is the only question.

SKYLARK

In practice

— 5 —

Set out with a positive, clear idea of *what you want* to achieve (and be realistic here) and by *when*. This way, you can start to play in a good frame of mind, knowing that the immediate goals are not only possible, but that you could also exceed them! Interestingly, you could start to become aware that you're enjoying the practice time more and more.

– 6 –

Have a warm-up first! Treat yourself like an athlete, and use plenty of stretching for your back, shoulders, arms and hands. Scales and studies are much better and rewarding if they go slowly first enabling the player to relax, and as a result there's much less chance of developing any unwelcome tension.

– 7 –

Stopping at hurdles starts to become habit-forming, but can be sorted very effectively. If you find that there *are* some hurdles, stop for a moment and realistically decide how to get over or around them. If you do not believe that you have the skill to tackle an obstacle, then find someone that does.

It could be that you gave yourself a dodgy deadline on something that had more to it than you thought at the time. Bear this in mind for your next deadline, and perhaps building in a little more slack could be one approach – but

In practice

there are many more solutions.

A sense of humour is a good start (if the cello is sounding more like a cat than Casals, then thank your lucky stars it wasn't sounding like a frog… etc)! Ask for advice from friends if you can – and try using a different method.

If all else fails, laugh, bypass the section (which by now has been earmarked as a spaghetti junction for the teacher) and play something else!

– 8 –

Always aim to finish on a high. Avoid stopping on a bit that you're finding difficult; instead, change to a couple of bars that you play really well and *leave it there*. Astonishingly, your **body** will remember the feeling, as well as your brain! When you look forward to beginning your next practice remember the *feeling* of playing well and it'll *feel* that much better for it.

Your muscles will relax and adapt for you far more readily as they will click in to the (good) memory of the last time that you played.

What a win, win situation!

Compare that to a feeling of tension and stress as you played something for the umpteenth time after 'keeping going until it's right' and it still sounded no better (in fact possibly worse)… and then you stopped. How would the next practice session start then?

– 9 –

Common problems.
a. The cello has just gone right out of tune. This is only a problem if the student is a beginner, and no one else in the house knows how to tune a cello. Practising with an instrument in this state will make things worse, not better, so get help – and quickly! I would *far* rather spend five minutes of my time as a teacher carefully tuning up a student's cello and get a decent week's

In practice

worth of practice as a result than refuse to do it for them – although I would put in a disclaimer on a string breaking first! Alternatively, ring another student who is more advanced (but be clear who settles if a string should snap) and remember that they are doing *you* a favour, not the other way around.

b. Make sure that your practising is not disturbed. It is really hard to concentrate if somebody comes careering through the room, or maybe worse when they creep through or stick around using the 'you won't notice me, I'll be so quiet' method. Both are attention getting, and need to be avoided!

> Every day, in every way, I am getting better and better.
> *Émile Coué*

c. *Parents and guardians*, beware of placing a child, a telly and a cello in the same room... the telly will win, and incidentally, the same goes for a computer and/or playstation!

Distractions can be outside too, for children. If friends are playing noisily below the window, that is quite simply *unfair* on any kid — better to move the friends, or delay their play until quarter-of-an-hour later using as much skulduggery as necessary.

d. *Illness*. Everybody gets ill from time to time, and that is when you should take it easy — and have *carte blanche* to enjoy listening to as much music that contains a cello as you like — without having the need to focus on it! Your playing and understanding of the instrument will then

In practice

benefit tremendously from the break, and you'll have that bit more musical experience under your belt – for no effort!

To conclude: it is very easy to start playing with all good intentions of playing for x amount of time every day. As long as the pointers above are taken into account, and to a certain extent followed (and no, it doesn't have to be *exactly*!) you can enjoy keeping all those good intentions and getting better at playing, enjoying your music, and – best of all – earning some well-merited praise not only from your teacher, whoever foots the bill, but also most of all – yourself!

CELLOTUDE

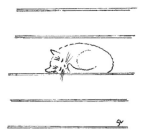

Notes

COMING SOON

Look out for further titles in

Sara Lovell's

Star Guides

The second in the series,

Solotude
igniting the flare in performance
(ISBN 1905636075 / 9781905636075)
is published in March 2007

BEAUTIFULBOOKS